This book belongs to

.....Naz...

....

You are capable of
amazing things.

Planner

SUNDAY	MONDAY	TUESDAY	WEDNESDAY
	8th NOV: HISTORY ASSESS-MENT; NOTES TO BE COMPLETED for NEXT DAY.	9th NOV: History assess-ment; in class;	

Month November 2021

THURSDAY	FRIDAY	SATURDAY	NOTES
			-) History → Remember to take notes in class for assessment

Weekly Schedule

TIME	MON	TUE	WED	THU	FRI
7:00 AM					
7:30 AM					
8:00 AM					
8:30 AM					
9:00 AM					
9:30 AM					
10:00 AM					
10:30 AM					
11:00 AM					
11:30 AM					
12:00 PM					
12:30 PM					
1:00 PM					
1:30 PM					
2:00 PM					
2:30 PM					
3:00 PM					
3:30 PM					
4:00 PM					
4:30 PM					
5:00 PM					
5:30 PM					
6:00 PM					
6:30 PM					
7:00 PM					
7:30 PM					

Daily Notes

Monday

Tuesday

Wednesday

Comms + Literature with Alison

Thursday

Friday

Saturday

Sunday

Notes

Weekly Schedule

TIME	MON	TUE	WED	THU	FRI
7:00 AM					
7:30 AM					
8:00 AM					
8:30 AM					
9:00 AM					
9:30 AM					
10:00 AM					
10:30 AM					
11:00 AM					
11:30 AM					
12:00 PM					
12:30 PM					
1:00 PM					
1:30 PM					
2:00 PM					
2:30 PM					
3:00 PM					
3:30 PM					
4:00 PM					
4:30 PM					
5:00 PM					
5:30 PM					
6:00 PM					
6:30 PM					
7:00 PM					
7:30 PM					

Daily Notes

Monday

Tuesday

Wednesday

Thursday

Friday

Saturday

Sunday

Notes

Weekly Schedule

TIME	MON	TUE	WED	THU	FRI
7:00 AM					
7:30 AM					
8:00 AM					
8:30 AM					
9:00 AM					
9:30 AM					
10:00 AM					
10:30 AM					
11:00 AM					
11:30 AM					
12:00 PM					
12:30 PM					
1:00 PM					
1:30 PM					
2:00 PM					
2:30 PM					
3:00 PM					
3:30 PM					
4:00 PM					
4:30 PM					
5:00 PM					
5:30 PM					
6:00 PM					
6:30 PM					
7:00 PM					
7:30 PM					

Daily Notes

Monday

Tuesday

Wednesday

Thursday

Friday

Saturday

Sunday

Notes

Weekly Schedule

TIME	MON	TUE	WED	THU	FRI
7:00 AM					
7:30 AM					
8:00 AM					
8:30 AM					
9:00 AM					
9:30 AM					
10:00 AM					
10:30 AM					
11:00 AM					
11:30 AM					
12:00 PM					
12:30 PM					
1:00 PM					
1:30 PM					
2:00 PM					
2:30 PM					
3:00 PM					
3:30 PM					
4:00 PM					
4:30 PM					
5:00 PM					
5:30 PM					
6:00 PM					
6:30 PM					
7:00 PM					
7:30 PM					

Daily Notes

Monday

Tuesday

Wednesday

Thursday

Friday

Saturday

Sunday

Notes

Weekly Schedule

TIME	MON	TUE	WED	THU	FRI
7:00 AM					
7:30 AM					
8:00 AM					
8:30 AM					
9:00 AM					
9:30 AM					
10:00 AM					
10:30 AM					
11:00 AM					
11:30 AM					
12:00 PM					
12:30 PM					
1:00 PM					
1:30 PM					
2:00 PM					
2:30 PM					
3:00 PM					
3:30 PM					
4:00 PM					
4:30 PM					
5:00 PM					
5:30 PM					
6:00 PM					
6:30 PM					
7:00 PM					
7:30 PM					

Daily Notes

Monday

Tuesday

Wednesday

Thursday

Friday

Saturday

Sunday

Notes

Planner

SUNDAY	MONDAY	TUESDAY	WEDNESDAY

Month

THURSDAY	FRIDAY	SATURDAY	NOTES

Weekly Schedule

TIME	MON	TUE	WED	THU	FRI
7:00 AM					
7:30 AM					
8:00 AM					
8:30 AM					
9:00 AM					
9:30 AM					
10:00 AM					
10:30 AM					
11:00 AM					
11:30 AM					
12:00 PM					
12:30 PM					
1:00 PM					
1:30 PM					
2:00 PM					
2:30 PM					
3:00 PM					
3:30 PM					
4:00 PM					
4:30 PM					
5:00 PM					
5:30 PM					
6:00 PM					
6:30 PM					
7:00 PM					
7:30 PM					

Daily Notes

Monday

Tuesday

Wednesday

Thursday

Friday

Saturday

Sunday

Notes

Weekly Schedule

TIME	MON	TUE	WED	THU	FRI
7:00 AM					
7:30 AM					
8:00 AM					
8:30 AM					
9:00 AM					
9:30 AM					
10:00 AM					
10:30 AM					
11:00 AM					
11:30 AM					
12:00 PM					
12:30 PM					
1:00 PM					
1:30 PM					
2:00 PM					
2:30 PM					
3:00 PM					
3:30 PM					
4:00 PM					
4:30 PM					
5:00 PM					
5:30 PM					
6:00 PM					
6:30 PM					
7:00 PM					
7:30 PM					

Daily Notes

Monday

Tuesday

Wednesday

Thursday

Friday

Saturday

Sunday

Notes

Weekly Schedule

TIME	MON	TUE	WED	THU	FRI
7:00 AM					
7:30 AM					
8:00 AM					
8:30 AM					
9:00 AM					
9:30 AM					
10:00 AM					
10:30 AM					
11:00 AM					
11:30 AM					
12:00 PM					
12:30 PM					
1:00 PM					
1:30 PM					
2:00 PM					
2:30 PM					
3:00 PM					
3:30 PM					
4:00 PM					
4:30 PM					
5:00 PM					
5:30 PM					
6:00 PM					
6:30 PM					
7:00 PM					
7:30 PM					

Daily Notes

Monday

Tuesday

Wednesday

Thursday

Friday

Saturday

Sunday

Notes

Weekly Schedule

TIME	MON	TUE	WED	THU	FRI
7:00 AM					
7:30 AM					
8:00 AM					
8:30 AM					
9:00 AM					
9:30 AM					
10:00 AM					
10:30 AM					
11:00 AM					
11:30 AM					
12:00 PM					
12:30 PM					
1:00 PM					
1:30 PM					
2:00 PM					
2:30 PM					
3:00 PM					
3:30 PM					
4:00 PM					
4:30 PM					
5:00 PM					
5:30 PM					
6:00 PM					
6:30 PM					
7:00 PM					
7:30 PM					

Daily Notes

Monday

Tuesday

Wednesday

Thursday

Friday

Saturday

Sunday

Notes

Weekly Schedule

TIME	MON	TUE	WED	THU	FRI
7:00 AM					
7:30 AM					
8:00 AM					
8:30 AM					
9:00 AM					
9:30 AM					
10:00 AM					
10:30 AM					
11:00 AM					
11:30 AM					
12:00 PM					
12:30 PM					
1:00 PM					
1:30 PM					
2:00 PM					
2:30 PM					
3:00 PM					
3:30 PM					
4:00 PM					
4:30 PM					
5:00 PM					
5:30 PM					
6:00 PM					
6:30 PM					
7:00 PM					
7:30 PM					

Daily Notes

Monday

Tuesday

Wednesday

Thursday

Friday

Saturday

Sunday

Notes

Planner

SUNDAY	MONDAY	TUESDAY	WEDNESDAY

# Month ....

THURSDAY	FRIDAY	SATURDAY	NOTES

Weekly Schedule

TIME	MON	TUE	WED	THU	FRI
7:00 AM					
7:30 AM					
8:00 AM					
8:30 AM					
9:00 AM					
9:30 AM					
10:00 AM					
10:30 AM					
11:00 AM					
11:30 AM					
12:00 PM					
12:30 PM					
1:00 PM					
1:30 PM					
2:00 PM					
2:30 PM					
3:00 PM					
3:30 PM					
4:00 PM					
4:30 PM					
5:00 PM					
5:30 PM					
6:00 PM					
6:30 PM					
7:00 PM					
7:30 PM					

Daily Notes

Monday

Tuesday

Wednesday

Thursday

Friday

Saturday

Sunday

Notes

Weekly Schedule

TIME	MON	TUE	WED	THU	FRI
7:00 AM					
7:30 AM					
8:00 AM					
8:30 AM					
9:00 AM					
9:30 AM					
10:00 AM					
10:30 AM					
11:00 AM					
11:30 AM					
12:00 PM					
12:30 PM					
1:00 PM					
1:30 PM					
2:00 PM					
2:30 PM					
3:00 PM					
3:30 PM					
4:00 PM					
4:30 PM					
5:00 PM					
5:30 PM					
6:00 PM					
6:30 PM					
7:00 PM					
7:30 PM					

Daily Notes

Monday

Tuesday

Wednesday

Thursday

Friday

Saturday

Sunday

Notes

Weekly Schedule

TIME	MON	TUE	WED	THU	FRI
7:00 AM					
7:30 AM					
8:00 AM					
8:30 AM					
9:00 AM					
9:30 AM					
10:00 AM					
10:30 AM					
11:00 AM					
11:30 AM					
12:00 PM					
12:30 PM					
1:00 PM					
1:30 PM					
2:00 PM					
2:30 PM					
3:00 PM					
3:30 PM					
4:00 PM					
4:30 PM					
5:00 PM					
5:30 PM					
6:00 PM					
6:30 PM					
7:00 PM					
7:30 PM					

Daily Notes

Monday

Tuesday

Wednesday

Thursday

Friday

Saturday

Sunday

Notes

Weekly Schedule

TIME	MON	TUE	WED	THU	FRI
7:00 AM					
7:30 AM					
8:00 AM					
8:30 AM					
9:00 AM					
9:30 AM					
10:00 AM					
10:30 AM					
11:00 AM					
11:30 AM					
12:00 PM					
12:30 PM					
1:00 PM					
1:30 PM					
2:00 PM					
2:30 PM					
3:00 PM					
3:30 PM					
4:00 PM					
4:30 PM					
5:00 PM					
5:30 PM					
6:00 PM					
6:30 PM					
7:00 PM					
7:30 PM					

Daily Notes

Monday

Tuesday

Wednesday

Thursday

Friday

Saturday

Sunday

Notes

Weekly Schedule

TIME	MON	TUE	WED	THU	FRI
7:00 AM					
7:30 AM					
8:00 AM					
8:30 AM					
9:00 AM					
9:30 AM					
10:00 AM					
10:30 AM					
11:00 AM					
11:30 AM					
12:00 PM					
12:30 PM					
1:00 PM					
1:30 PM					
2:00 PM					
2:30 PM					
3:00 PM					
3:30 PM					
4:00 PM					
4:30 PM					
5:00 PM					
5:30 PM					
6:00 PM					
6:30 PM					
7:00 PM					
7:30 PM					

Daily Notes

Monday

Tuesday

Wednesday

Thursday

Friday

Saturday

Sunday

Notes

Planner

SUNDAY	MONDAY	TUESDAY	WEDNESDAY

THURSDAY	FRIDAY	SATURDAY	NOTES

Weekly Schedule

TIME	MON	TUE	WED	THU	FRI
7:00 AM					
7:30 AM					
8:00 AM					
8:30 AM					
9:00 AM					
9:30 AM					
10:00 AM					
10:30 AM					
11:00 AM					
11:30 AM					
12:00 PM					
12:30 PM					
1:00 PM					
1:30 PM					
2:00 PM					
2:30 PM					
3:00 PM					
3:30 PM					
4:00 PM					
4:30 PM					
5:00 PM					
5:30 PM					
6:00 PM					
6:30 PM					
7:00 PM					
7:30 PM					

Daily Notes

Monday

Tuesday

Wednesday

Thursday

Friday

Saturday

Sunday

Notes

Weekly Schedule

TIME	MON	TUE	WED	THU	FRI
7:00 AM					
7:30 AM					
8:00 AM					
8:30 AM					
9:00 AM					
9:30 AM					
10:00 AM					
10:30 AM					
11:00 AM					
11:30 AM					
12:00 PM					
12:30 PM					
1:00 PM					
1:30 PM					
2:00 PM					
2:30 PM					
3:00 PM					
3:30 PM					
4:00 PM					
4:30 PM					
5:00 PM					
5:30 PM					
6:00 PM					
6:30 PM					
7:00 PM					
7:30 PM					

Daily Notes

Monday

Tuesday

Wednesday

Thursday

Friday

Saturday

Sunday

Notes

Weekly Schedule

TIME	MON	TUE	WED	THU	FRI
7:00 AM					
7:30 AM					
8:00 AM					
8:30 AM					
9:00 AM					
9:30 AM					
10:00 AM					
10:30 AM					
11:00 AM					
11:30 AM					
12:00 PM					
12:30 PM					
1:00 PM					
1:30 PM					
2:00 PM					
2:30 PM					
3:00 PM					
3:30 PM					
4:00 PM					
4:30 PM					
5:00 PM					
5:30 PM					
6:00 PM					
6:30 PM					
7:00 PM					
7:30 PM					

Daily Notes

Monday

Tuesday

Wednesday

Thursday

Friday

Saturday

Sunday

Notes

Weekly Schedule

TIME	MON	TUE	WED	THU	FRI
7:00 AM					
7:30 AM					
8:00 AM					
8:30 AM					
9:00 AM					
9:30 AM					
10:00 AM					
10:30 AM					
11:00 AM					
11:30 AM					
12:00 PM					
12:30 PM					
1:00 PM					
1:30 PM					
2:00 PM					
2:30 PM					
3:00 PM					
3:30 PM					
4:00 PM					
4:30 PM					
5:00 PM					
5:30 PM					
6:00 PM					
6:30 PM					
7:00 PM					
7:30 PM					

Daily Notes

Monday

Tuesday

Wednesday

Thursday

Friday

Saturday

Sunday

Notes

Weekly Schedule

TIME	MON	TUE	WED	THU	FRI
7:00 AM					
7:30 AM					
8:00 AM					
8:30 AM					
9:00 AM					
9:30 AM					
10:00 AM					
10:30 AM					
11:00 AM					
11:30 AM					
12:00 PM					
12:30 PM					
1:00 PM					
1:30 PM					
2:00 PM					
2:30 PM					
3:00 PM					
3:30 PM					
4:00 PM					
4:30 PM					
5:00 PM					
5:30 PM					
6:00 PM					
6:30 PM					
7:00 PM					
7:30 PM					

Daily Notes

Monday

Tuesday

Wednesday

Thursday

Friday

Saturday

Sunday

Notes

Planner

SUNDAY	MONDAY	TUESDAY	WEDNESDAY

THURSDAY	FRIDAY	SATURDAY	NOTES

Weekly Schedule

TIME	MON	TUE	WED	THU	FRI
7:00 AM					
7:30 AM					
8:00 AM					
8:30 AM					
9:00 AM					
9:30 AM					
10:00 AM					
10:30 AM					
11:00 AM					
11:30 AM					
12:00 PM					
12:30 PM					
1:00 PM					
1:30 PM					
2:00 PM					
2:30 PM					
3:00 PM					
3:30 PM					
4:00 PM					
4:30 PM					
5:00 PM					
5:30 PM					
6:00 PM					
6:30 PM					
7:00 PM					
7:30 PM					

Daily Notes

Monday

Tuesday

Wednesday

Thursday

Friday

Saturday

Sunday

Notes

Weekly Schedule

TIME	MON	TUE	WED	THU	FRI
7:00 AM					
7:30 AM					
8:00 AM					
8:30 AM					
9:00 AM					
9:30 AM					
10:00 AM					
10:30 AM					
11:00 AM					
11:30 AM					
12:00 PM					
12:30 PM					
1:00 PM					
1:30 PM					
2:00 PM					
2:30 PM					
3:00 PM					
3:30 PM					
4:00 PM					
4:30 PM					
5:00 PM					
5:30 PM					
6:00 PM					
6:30 PM					
7:00 PM					
7:30 PM					

Daily Notes

Monday

Tuesday

Wednesday

Thursday

Friday

Saturday

Sunday

Notes

Weekly Schedule

TIME	MON	TUE	WED	THU	FRI
7:00 AM					
7:30 AM					
8:00 AM					
8:30 AM					
9:00 AM					
9:30 AM					
10:00 AM					
10:30 AM					
11:00 AM					
11:30 AM					
12:00 PM					
12:30 PM					
1:00 PM					
1:30 PM					
2:00 PM					
2:30 PM					
3:00 PM					
3:30 PM					
4:00 PM					
4:30 PM					
5:00 PM					
5:30 PM					
6:00 PM					
6:30 PM					
7:00 PM					
7:30 PM					

Daily Notes

Monday

Tuesday

Wednesday

Thursday

Friday

Saturday

Sunday

Notes

Weekly Schedule

TIME	MON	TUE	WED	THU	FRI
7:00 AM					
7:30 AM					
8:00 AM					
8:30 AM					
9:00 AM					
9:30 AM					
10:00 AM					
10:30 AM					
11:00 AM					
11:30 AM					
12:00 PM					
12:30 PM					
1:00 PM					
1:30 PM					
2:00 PM					
2:30 PM					
3:00 PM					
3:30 PM					
4:00 PM					
4:30 PM					
5:00 PM					
5:30 PM					
6:00 PM					
6:30 PM					
7:00 PM					
7:30 PM					

Daily Notes

Monday

Tuesday

Wednesday

Thursday

Friday

Saturday

Sunday

Notes

Weekly Schedule

TIME	MON	TUE	WED	THU	FRI
7:00 AM					
7:30 AM					
8:00 AM					
8:30 AM					
9:00 AM					
9:30 AM					
10:00 AM					
10:30 AM					
11:00 AM					
11:30 AM					
12:00 PM					
12:30 PM					
1:00 PM					
1:30 PM					
2:00 PM					
2:30 PM					
3:00 PM					
3:30 PM					
4:00 PM					
4:30 PM					
5:00 PM					
5:30 PM					
6:00 PM					
6:30 PM					
7:00 PM					
7:30 PM					

Daily Notes

Monday

Tuesday

Wednesday

Thursday

Friday

Saturday

Sunday

Notes

SUNDAY	MONDAY	TUESDAY	WEDNESDAY

THURSDAY	FRIDAY	SATURDAY	NOTES

Weekly Schedule

TIME	MON	TUE	WED	THU	FRI
7:00 AM					
7:30 AM					
8:00 AM					
8:30 AM					
9:00 AM					
9:30 AM					
10:00 AM					
10:30 AM					
11:00 AM					
11:30 AM					
12:00 PM					
12:30 PM					
1:00 PM					
1:30 PM					
2:00 PM					
2:30 PM					
3:00 PM					
3:30 PM					
4:00 PM					
4:30 PM					
5:00 PM					
5:30 PM					
6:00 PM					
6:30 PM					
7:00 PM					
7:30 PM					

Daily Notes

Monday

Tuesday

Wednesday

Thursday

Friday

Saturday

Sunday

Notes

Weekly Schedule

TIME	MON	TUE	WED	THU	FRI
7:00 AM					
7:30 AM					
8:00 AM					
8:30 AM					
9:00 AM					
9:30 AM					
10:00 AM					
10:30 AM					
11:00 AM					
11:30 AM					
12:00 PM					
12:30 PM					
1:00 PM					
1:30 PM					
2:00 PM					
2:30 PM					
3:00 PM					
3:30 PM					
4:00 PM					
4:30 PM					
5:00 PM					
5:30 PM					
6:00 PM					
6:30 PM					
7:00 PM					
7:30 PM					

Daily Notes

Monday

Tuesday

Wednesday

Thursday

Friday

Saturday

Sunday

Notes

Weekly Schedule

TIME	MON	TUE	WED	THU	FRI
7:00 AM					
7:30 AM					
8:00 AM					
8:30 AM					
9:00 AM					
9:30 AM					
10:00 AM					
10:30 AM					
11:00 AM					
11:30 AM					
12:00 PM					
12:30 PM					
1:00 PM					
1:30 PM					
2:00 PM					
2:30 PM					
3:00 PM					
3:30 PM					
4:00 PM					
4:30 PM					
5:00 PM					
5:30 PM					
6:00 PM					
6:30 PM					
7:00 PM					
7:30 PM					

Daily Notes

Monday

Tuesday

Wednesday

Thursday

Friday

Saturday

Sunday

Notes

Weekly Schedule

TIME	MON	TUE	WED	THU	FRI
7:00 AM					
7:30 AM					
8:00 AM					
8:30 AM					
9:00 AM					
9:30 AM					
10:00 AM					
10:30 AM					
11:00 AM					
11:30 AM					
12:00 PM					
12:30 PM					
1:00 PM					
1:30 PM					
2:00 PM					
2:30 PM					
3:00 PM					
3:30 PM					
4:00 PM					
4:30 PM					
5:00 PM					
5:30 PM					
6:00 PM					
6:30 PM					
7:00 PM					
7:30 PM					

Daily Notes

Monday

Tuesday

Wednesday

Thursday

Friday

Saturday

Sunday

Notes

Weekly Schedule

TIME	MON	TUE	WED	THU	FRI
7:00 AM					
7:30 AM					
8:00 AM					
8:30 AM					
9:00 AM					
9:30 AM					
10:00 AM					
10:30 AM					
11:00 AM					
11:30 AM					
12:00 PM					
12:30 PM					
1:00 PM					
1:30 PM					
2:00 PM					
2:30 PM					
3:00 PM					
3:30 PM					
4:00 PM					
4:30 PM					
5:00 PM					
5:30 PM					
6:00 PM					
6:30 PM					
7:00 PM					
7:30 PM					

Daily Notes

Monday

Tuesday

Wednesday

Thursday

Friday

Saturday

Sunday

Notes

SUNDAY	MONDAY	TUESDAY	WEDNESDAY

THURSDAY	FRIDAY	SATURDAY	NOTES

Weekly Schedule

TIME	MON	TUE	WED	THU	FRI
7:00 AM					
7:30 AM					
8:00 AM					
8:30 AM					
9:00 AM					
9:30 AM					
10:00 AM					
10:30 AM					
11:00 AM					
11:30 AM					
12:00 PM					
12:30 PM					
1:00 PM					
1:30 PM					
2:00 PM					
2:30 PM					
3:00 PM					
3:30 PM					
4:00 PM					
4:30 PM					
5:00 PM					
5:30 PM					
6:00 PM					
6:30 PM					
7:00 PM					
7:30 PM					

Daily Notes

Monday

Tuesday

Wednesday

Thursday

Friday

Saturday

Sunday

Notes

Weekly Schedule

TIME	MON	TUE	WED	THU	FRI
7:00 AM					
7:30 AM					
8:00 AM					
8:30 AM					
9:00 AM					
9:30 AM					
10:00 AM					
10:30 AM					
11:00 AM					
11:30 AM					
12:00 PM					
12:30 PM					
1:00 PM					
1:30 PM					
2:00 PM					
2:30 PM					
3:00 PM					
3:30 PM					
4:00 PM					
4:30 PM					
5:00 PM					
5:30 PM					
6:00 PM					
6:30 PM					
7:00 PM					
7:30 PM					

Daily Notes

Monday

Tuesday

Wednesday

Thursday

Friday

Saturday

Sunday

Notes

Weekly Schedule

TIME	MON	TUE	WED	THU	FRI
7:00 AM					
7:30 AM					
8:00 AM					
8:30 AM					
9:00 AM					
9:30 AM					
10:00 AM					
10:30 AM					
11:00 AM					
11:30 AM					
12:00 PM					
12:30 PM					
1:00 PM					
1:30 PM					
2:00 PM					
2:30 PM					
3:00 PM					
3:30 PM					
4:00 PM					
4:30 PM					
5:00 PM					
5:30 PM					
6:00 PM					
6:30 PM					
7:00 PM					
7:30 PM					

Daily Notes

Monday

Tuesday

Wednesday

Thursday

Friday

Saturday

Sunday

Notes

Weekly Schedule

TIME	MON	TUE	WED	THU	FRI
7:00 AM					
7:30 AM					
8:00 AM					
8:30 AM					
9:00 AM					
9:30 AM					
10:00 AM					
10:30 AM					
11:00 AM					
11:30 AM					
12:00 PM					
12:30 PM					
1:00 PM					
1:30 PM					
2:00 PM					
2:30 PM					
3:00 PM					
3:30 PM					
4:00 PM					
4:30 PM					
5:00 PM					
5:30 PM					
6:00 PM					
6:30 PM					
7:00 PM					
7:30 PM					

Daily Notes

Monday

Tuesday

Wednesday

Thursday

Friday

Saturday

Sunday

Notes

Weekly Schedule

TIME	MON	TUE	WED	THU	FRI
7:00 AM					
7:30 AM					
8:00 AM					
8:30 AM					
9:00 AM					
9:30 AM					
10:00 AM					
10:30 AM					
11:00 AM					
11:30 AM					
12:00 PM					
12:30 PM					
1:00 PM					
1:30 PM					
2:00 PM					
2:30 PM					
3:00 PM					
3:30 PM					
4:00 PM					
4:30 PM					
5:00 PM					
5:30 PM					
6:00 PM					
6:30 PM					
7:00 PM					
7:30 PM					

Daily Notes

Monday

Tuesday

Wednesday

Thursday

Friday

Saturday

Sunday

Notes

 Planner

SUNDAY	MONDAY	TUESDAY	WEDNESDAY

THURSDAY	FRIDAY	SATURDAY	NOTES

Weekly Schedule

TIME	MON	TUE	WED	THU	FRI
7:00 AM					
7:30 AM					
8:00 AM					
8:30 AM					
9:00 AM					
9:30 AM					
10:00 AM					
10:30 AM					
11:00 AM					
11:30 AM					
12:00 PM					
12:30 PM					
1:00 PM					
1:30 PM					
2:00 PM					
2:30 PM					
3:00 PM					
3:30 PM					
4:00 PM					
4:30 PM					
5:00 PM					
5:30 PM					
6:00 PM					
6:30 PM					
7:00 PM					
7:30 PM					

Daily Notes

Monday

Tuesday

Wednesday

Thursday

Friday

Saturday

Sunday

Notes

Weekly Schedule

TIME	MON	TUE	WED	THU	FRI
7:00 AM					
7:30 AM					
8:00 AM					
8:30 AM					
9:00 AM					
9:30 AM					
10:00 AM					
10:30 AM					
11:00 AM					
11:30 AM					
12:00 PM					
12:30 PM					
1:00 PM					
1:30 PM					
2:00 PM					
2:30 PM					
3:00 PM					
3:30 PM					
4:00 PM					
4:30 PM					
5:00 PM					
5:30 PM					
6:00 PM					
6:30 PM					
7:00 PM					
7:30 PM					

Daily Notes

Monday

Tuesday

Wednesday

Thursday

Friday

Saturday

Sunday

Notes

Weekly Schedule

TIME	MON	TUE	WED	THU	FRI
7:00 AM					
7:30 AM					
8:00 AM					
8:30 AM					
9:00 AM					
9:30 AM					
10:00 AM					
10:30 AM					
11:00 AM					
11:30 AM					
12:00 PM					
12:30 PM					
1:00 PM					
1:30 PM					
2:00 PM					
2:30 PM					
3:00 PM					
3:30 PM					
4:00 PM					
4:30 PM					
5:00 PM					
5:30 PM					
6:00 PM					
6:30 PM					
7:00 PM					
7:30 PM					

Daily Notes

Monday

Tuesday

Wednesday

Thursday

Friday

Saturday

Sunday

Notes

Weekly Schedule

TIME	MON	TUE	WED	THU	FRI
7:00 AM					
7:30 AM					
8:00 AM					
8:30 AM					
9:00 AM					
9:30 AM					
10:00 AM					
10:30 AM					
11:00 AM					
11:30 AM					
12:00 PM					
12:30 PM					
1:00 PM					
1:30 PM					
2:00 PM					
2:30 PM					
3:00 PM					
3:30 PM					
4:00 PM					
4:30 PM					
5:00 PM					
5:30 PM					
6:00 PM					
6:30 PM					
7:00 PM					
7:30 PM					

Daily Notes

Monday

Tuesday

Wednesday

Thursday

Friday

Saturday

Sunday

Notes

Weekly Schedule

TIME	MON	TUE	WED	THU	FRI
7:00 AM					
7:30 AM					
8:00 AM					
8:30 AM					
9:00 AM					
9:30 AM					
10:00 AM					
10:30 AM					
11:00 AM					
11:30 AM					
12:00 PM					
12:30 PM					
1:00 PM					
1:30 PM					
2:00 PM					
2:30 PM					
3:00 PM					
3:30 PM					
4:00 PM					
4:30 PM					
5:00 PM					
5:30 PM					
6:00 PM					
6:30 PM					
7:00 PM					
7:30 PM					

Daily Notes

Monday

Tuesday

Wednesday

Thursday

Friday

Saturday

Sunday

Notes

SUNDAY	MONDAY	TUESDAY	WEDNESDAY

THURSDAY	FRIDAY	SATURDAY	NOTES

Weekly Schedule

TIME	MON	TUE	WED	THU	FRI
7:00 AM					
7:30 AM					
8:00 AM					
8:30 AM					
9:00 AM					
9:30 AM					
10:00 AM					
10:30 AM					
11:00 AM					
11:30 AM					
12:00 PM					
12:30 PM					
1:00 PM					
1:30 PM					
2:00 PM					
2:30 PM					
3:00 PM					
3:30 PM					
4:00 PM					
4:30 PM					
5:00 PM					
5:30 PM					
6:00 PM					
6:30 PM					
7:00 PM					
7:30 PM					

Daily Notes

Monday

Tuesday

Wednesday

Thursday

Friday

Saturday

Sunday

Notes

Weekly Schedule

TIME	MON	TUE	WED	THU	FRI
7:00 AM					
7:30 AM					
8:00 AM					
8:30 AM					
9:00 AM					
9:30 AM					
10:00 AM					
10:30 AM					
11:00 AM					
11:30 AM					
12:00 PM					
12:30 PM					
1:00 PM					
1:30 PM					
2:00 PM					
2:30 PM					
3:00 PM					
3:30 PM					
4:00 PM					
4:30 PM					
5:00 PM					
5:30 PM					
6:00 PM					
6:30 PM					
7:00 PM					
7:30 PM					

Daily Notes

Monday

Tuesday

Wednesday

Thursday

Friday

Saturday

Sunday

Notes

Weekly Schedule

TIME	MON	TUE	WED	THU	FRI
7:00 AM					
7:30 AM					
8:00 AM					
8:30 AM					
9:00 AM					
9:30 AM					
10:00 AM					
10:30 AM					
11:00 AM					
11:30 AM					
12:00 PM					
12:30 PM					
1:00 PM					
1:30 PM					
2:00 PM					
2:30 PM					
3:00 PM					
3:30 PM					
4:00 PM					
4:30 PM					
5:00 PM					
5:30 PM					
6:00 PM					
6:30 PM					
7:00 PM					
7:30 PM					

Daily Notes

Monday

Tuesday

Wednesday

Thursday

Friday

Saturday

Sunday

Notes

Weekly Schedule

TIME	MON	TUE	WED	THU	FRI
7:00 AM					
7:30 AM					
8:00 AM					
8:30 AM					
9:00 AM					
9:30 AM					
10:00 AM					
10:30 AM					
11:00 AM					
11:30 AM					
12:00 PM					
12:30 PM					
1:00 PM					
1:30 PM					
2:00 PM					
2:30 PM					
3:00 PM					
3:30 PM					
4:00 PM					
4:30 PM					
5:00 PM					
5:30 PM					
6:00 PM					
6:30 PM					
7:00 PM					
7:30 PM					

Daily Notes

Monday

Tuesday

Wednesday

Thursday

Friday

Saturday

Sunday

Notes

Weekly Schedule

TIME	MON	TUE	WED	THU	FRI
7:00 AM					
7:30 AM					
8:00 AM					
8:30 AM					
9:00 AM					
9:30 AM					
10:00 AM					
10:30 AM					
11:00 AM					
11:30 AM					
12:00 PM					
12:30 PM					
1:00 PM					
1:30 PM					
2:00 PM					
2:30 PM					
3:00 PM					
3:30 PM					
4:00 PM					
4:30 PM					
5:00 PM					
5:30 PM					
6:00 PM					
6:30 PM					
7:00 PM					
7:30 PM					

Daily Notes

Monday

Tuesday

Wednesday

Thursday

Friday

Saturday

Sunday

Notes

# Planner

SUNDAY	MONDAY	TUESDAY	WEDNESDAY

THURSDAY	FRIDAY	SATURDAY	NOTES

Weekly Schedule

TIME	MON	TUE	WED	THU	FRI
7:00 AM					
7:30 AM					
8:00 AM					
8:30 AM					
9:00 AM					
9:30 AM					
10:00 AM					
10:30 AM					
11:00 AM					
11:30 AM					
12:00 PM					
12:30 PM					
1:00 PM					
1:30 PM					
2:00 PM					
2:30 PM					
3:00 PM					
3:30 PM					
4:00 PM					
4:30 PM					
5:00 PM					
5:30 PM					
6:00 PM					
6:30 PM					
7:00 PM					
7:30 PM					

Daily Notes

Monday

Tuesday

Wednesday

Thursday

Friday

Saturday

Sunday

Notes

Weekly Schedule

TIME	MON	TUE	WED	THU	FRI
7:00 AM					
7:30 AM					
8:00 AM					
8:30 AM					
9:00 AM					
9:30 AM					
10:00 AM					
10:30 AM					
11:00 AM					
11:30 AM					
12:00 PM					
12:30 PM					
1:00 PM					
1:30 PM					
2:00 PM					
2:30 PM					
3:00 PM					
3:30 PM					
4:00 PM					
4:30 PM					
5:00 PM					
5:30 PM					
6:00 PM					
6:30 PM					
7:00 PM					
7:30 PM					

Daily Notes

Monday

Tuesday

Wednesday

Thursday

Friday

Saturday

Sunday

Notes

Weekly Schedule

TIME	MON	TUE	WED	THU	FRI
7:00 AM					
7:30 AM					
8:00 AM					
8:30 AM					
9:00 AM					
9:30 AM					
10:00 AM					
10:30 AM					
11:00 AM					
11:30 AM					
12:00 PM					
12:30 PM					
1:00 PM					
1:30 PM					
2:00 PM					
2:30 PM					
3:00 PM					
3:30 PM					
4:00 PM					
4:30 PM					
5:00 PM					
5:30 PM					
6:00 PM					
6:30 PM					
7:00 PM					
7:30 PM					

Daily Notes

Monday

Tuesday

Wednesday

Thursday

Friday

Saturday

Sunday

Notes

Weekly Schedule

TIME	MON	TUE	WED	THU	FRI
7:00 AM					
7:30 AM					
8:00 AM					
8:30 AM					
9:00 AM					
9:30 AM					
10:00 AM					
10:30 AM					
11:00 AM					
11:30 AM					
12:00 PM					
12:30 PM					
1:00 PM					
1:30 PM					
2:00 PM					
2:30 PM					
3:00 PM					
3:30 PM					
4:00 PM					
4:30 PM					
5:00 PM					
5:30 PM					
6:00 PM					
6:30 PM					
7:00 PM					
7:30 PM					

Daily Notes

Monday

Tuesday

Wednesday

Thursday

Friday

Saturday

Sunday

Notes

Weekly Schedule

TIME	MON	TUE	WED	THU	FRI
7:00 AM					
7:30 AM					
8:00 AM					
8:30 AM					
9:00 AM					
9:30 AM					
10:00 AM					
10:30 AM					
11:00 AM					
11:30 AM					
12:00 PM					
12:30 PM					
1:00 PM					
1:30 PM					
2:00 PM					
2:30 PM					
3:00 PM					
3:30 PM					
4:00 PM					
4:30 PM					
5:00 PM					
5:30 PM					
6:00 PM					
6:30 PM					
7:00 PM					
7:30 PM					

Daily Notes

Monday

Tuesday

Wednesday

Thursday

Friday

Saturday

Sunday

Notes

<table>
<tr><th>SUNDAY</th><th>MONDAY</th><th>TUESDAY</th><th>WEDNESDAY</th></tr>
</table>

THURSDAY	FRIDAY	SATURDAY	NOTES

Weekly Schedule

TIME	MON	TUE	WED	THU	FRI
7:00 AM					
7:30 AM					
8:00 AM					
8:30 AM					
9:00 AM					
9:30 AM					
10:00 AM					
10:30 AM					
11:00 AM					
11:30 AM					
12:00 PM					
12:30 PM					
1:00 PM					
1:30 PM					
2:00 PM					
2:30 PM					
3:00 PM					
3:30 PM					
4:00 PM					
4:30 PM					
5:00 PM					
5:30 PM					
6:00 PM					
6:30 PM					
7:00 PM					
7:30 PM					

Daily Notes

Monday

Tuesday

Wednesday

Thursday

Friday

Saturday

Sunday

Notes

Weekly Schedule

TIME	MON	TUE	WED	THU	FRI
7:00 AM					
7:30 AM					
8:00 AM					
8:30 AM					
9:00 AM					
9:30 AM					
10:00 AM					
10:30 AM					
11:00 AM					
11:30 AM					
12:00 PM					
12:30 PM					
1:00 PM					
1:30 PM					
2:00 PM					
2:30 PM					
3:00 PM					
3:30 PM					
4:00 PM					
4:30 PM					
5:00 PM					
5:30 PM					
6:00 PM					
6:30 PM					
7:00 PM					
7:30 PM					

Daily Notes

Monday

Tuesday

Wednesday

Thursday

Friday

Saturday

Sunday

Notes

Weekly Schedule

TIME	MON	TUE	WED	THU	FRI
7:00 AM					
7:30 AM					
8:00 AM					
8:30 AM					
9:00 AM					
9:30 AM					
10:00 AM					
10:30 AM					
11:00 AM					
11:30 AM					
12:00 PM					
12:30 PM					
1:00 PM					
1:30 PM					
2:00 PM					
2:30 PM					
3:00 PM					
3:30 PM					
4:00 PM					
4:30 PM					
5:00 PM					
5:30 PM					
6:00 PM					
6:30 PM					
7:00 PM					
7:30 PM					

Daily Notes

Monday

Tuesday

Wednesday

Thursday

Friday

Saturday

Sunday

Notes

Weekly Schedule

TIME	MON	TUE	WED	THU	FRI
7:00 AM					
7:30 AM					
8:00 AM					
8:30 AM					
9:00 AM					
9:30 AM					
10:00 AM					
10:30 AM					
11:00 AM					
11:30 AM					
12:00 PM					
12:30 PM					
1:00 PM					
1:30 PM					
2:00 PM					
2:30 PM					
3:00 PM					
3:30 PM					
4:00 PM					
4:30 PM					
5:00 PM					
5:30 PM					
6:00 PM					
6:30 PM					
7:00 PM					
7:30 PM					

Daily Notes

Monday

Tuesday

Wednesday

Thursday

Friday

Saturday

Sunday

Notes

Weekly Schedule

TIME	MON	TUE	WED	THU	FRI
7:00 AM					
7:30 AM					
8:00 AM					
8:30 AM					
9:00 AM					
9:30 AM					
10:00 AM					
10:30 AM					
11:00 AM					
11:30 AM					
12:00 PM					
12:30 PM					
1:00 PM					
1:30 PM					
2:00 PM					
2:30 PM					
3:00 PM					
3:30 PM					
4:00 PM					
4:30 PM					
5:00 PM					
5:30 PM					
6:00 PM					
6:30 PM					
7:00 PM					
7:30 PM					

Daily Notes

Monday

Tuesday

Wednesday

Thursday

Friday

Saturday

Sunday

Notes

Planner

SUNDAY	MONDAY	TUESDAY	WEDNESDAY

THURSDAY	FRIDAY	SATURDAY	NOTES

Weekly Schedule

TIME	MON	TUE	WED	THU	FRI
7:00 AM					
7:30 AM					
8:00 AM					
8:30 AM					
9:00 AM					
9:30 AM					
10:00 AM					
10:30 AM					
11:00 AM					
11:30 AM					
12:00 PM					
12:30 PM					
1:00 PM					
1:30 PM					
2:00 PM					
2:30 PM					
3:00 PM					
3:30 PM					
4:00 PM					
4:30 PM					
5:00 PM					
5:30 PM					
6:00 PM					
6:30 PM					
7:00 PM					
7:30 PM					

Daily Notes

Monday

Tuesday

Wednesday

Thursday

Friday

Saturday

Sunday

Notes

Weekly Schedule

TIME	MON	TUE	WED	THU	FRI
7:00 AM					
7:30 AM					
8:00 AM					
8:30 AM					
9:00 AM					
9:30 AM					
10:00 AM					
10:30 AM					
11:00 AM					
11:30 AM					
12:00 PM					
12:30 PM					
1:00 PM					
1:30 PM					
2:00 PM					
2:30 PM					
3:00 PM					
3:30 PM					
4:00 PM					
4:30 PM					
5:00 PM					
5:30 PM					
6:00 PM					
6:30 PM					
7:00 PM					
7:30 PM					

Daily Notes

Monday

Tuesday

Wednesday

Thursday

Friday

Saturday

Sunday

Notes

Weekly Schedule

TIME	MON	TUE	WED	THU	FRI
7:00 AM					
7:30 AM					
8:00 AM					
8:30 AM					
9:00 AM					
9:30 AM					
10:00 AM					
10:30 AM					
11:00 AM					
11:30 AM					
12:00 PM					
12:30 PM					
1:00 PM					
1:30 PM					
2:00 PM					
2:30 PM					
3:00 PM					
3:30 PM					
4:00 PM					
4:30 PM					
5:00 PM					
5:30 PM					
6:00 PM					
6:30 PM					
7:00 PM					
7:30 PM					

Daily Notes

Monday

Tuesday

Wednesday

Thursday

Friday

Saturday

Sunday

Notes

Weekly Schedule

TIME	MON	TUE	WED	THU	FRI
7:00 AM					
7:30 AM					
8:00 AM					
8:30 AM					
9:00 AM					
9:30 AM					
10:00 AM					
10:30 AM					
11:00 AM					
11:30 AM					
12:00 PM					
12:30 PM					
1:00 PM					
1:30 PM					
2:00 PM					
2:30 PM					
3:00 PM					
3:30 PM					
4:00 PM					
4:30 PM					
5:00 PM					
5:30 PM					
6:00 PM					
6:30 PM					
7:00 PM					
7:30 PM					

Daily Notes

Monday

Tuesday

Wednesday

Thursday

Friday

Saturday

Sunday

Notes

Weekly Schedule

TIME	MON	TUE	WED	THU	FRI
7:00 AM					
7:30 AM					
8:00 AM					
8:30 AM					
9:00 AM					
9:30 AM					
10:00 AM					
10:30 AM					
11:00 AM					
11:30 AM					
12:00 PM					
12:30 PM					
1:00 PM					
1:30 PM					
2:00 PM					
2:30 PM					
3:00 PM					
3:30 PM					
4:00 PM					
4:30 PM					
5:00 PM					
5:30 PM					
6:00 PM					
6:30 PM					
7:00 PM					
7:30 PM					

Daily Notes

Monday

Tuesday

Wednesday

Thursday

Friday

Saturday

Sunday

Notes

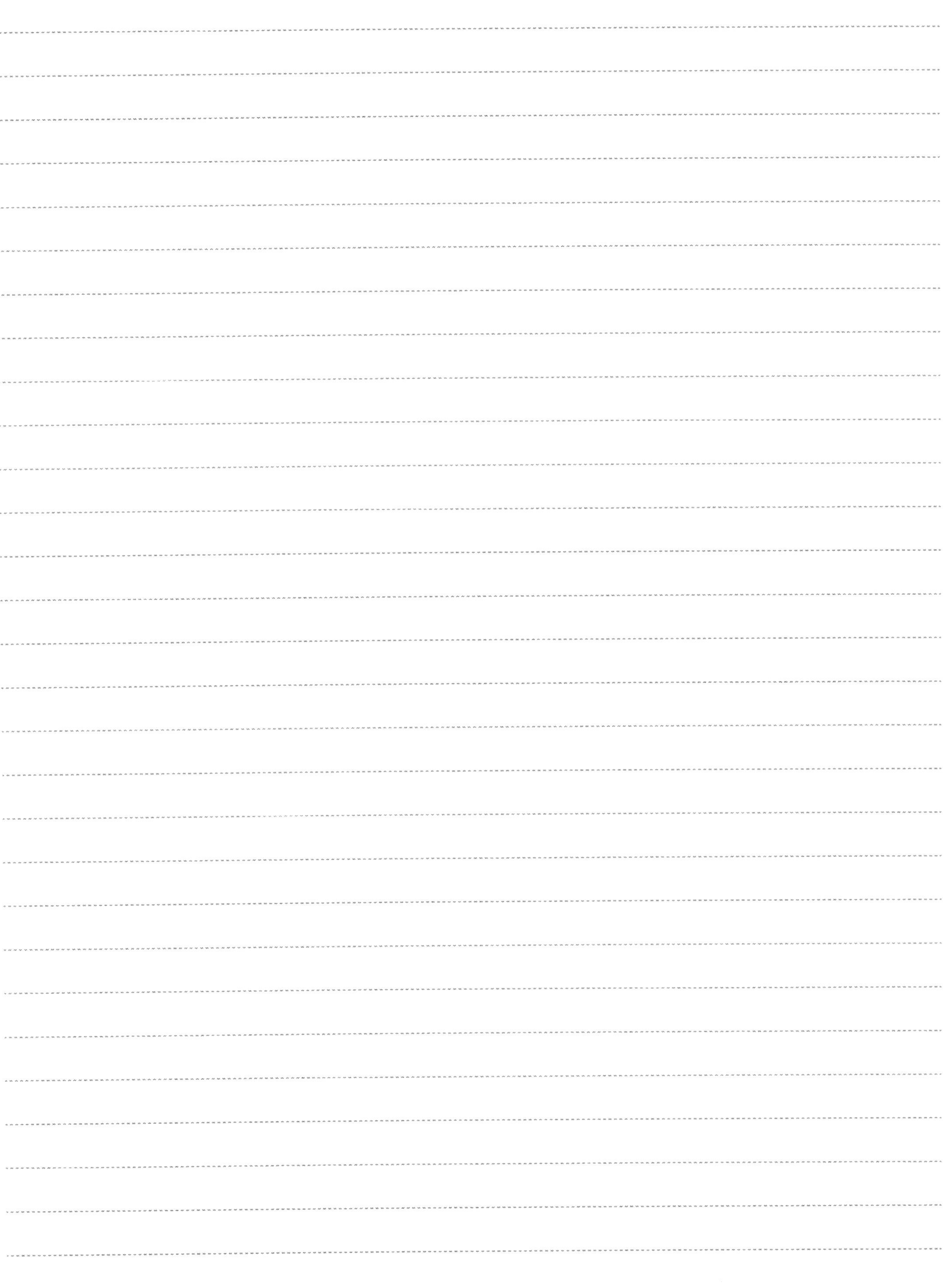

Printed in Great Britain
by Amazon